THE BOOK OF SNAKES

WELBECK
CHILDREN'S BOOKS

First published in 2025 by Welbeck Children's Books
An imprint of Hachette Children's Group
Copyright © 2025 Hodder & Stoughton Limited
Author: Brian Williams

All rights reserved. No part of this publication may be reproduced, stored in a retrieval system, or transmitted in any form or by any means, electronically, mechanical, photocopying, recording, or otherwise, without the prior permission of the copyright owners and the publishers.

ISBN 978 1 80453 676 6
Printed in Dongguan, China
10 9 8 7 6 5 4 3 2 1

Welbeck Children's Books
An imprint of Hachette Children's Group
Part of Hodder & Stoughton Limited
Carmelite House, 50 Victoria Embankment
London EC4Y 0DZ

An Hachette UK Company
www.hachette.co.uk
www.hachettechildrens.co.uk

MIX
Paper | Supporting responsible forestry
FSC® C104740

An Indian python with its jaws wide open

Coastal taipan

SAFETY WARNING
Although many snakes are harmless to people, and some can be kept as pets, others can be dangerous. All wild snakes should be left undisturbed.

Contents

CHAPTER 1

My snake explorer's notebook	4
Snakes and dinosaurs	6
Where in the world?	8
Pythons	10
Python habits	12
Boas	14
Colubrids	16
Vipers	18
Elapids	20

CHAPTER 2

Snake anatomy	22
Reticulated python	24
Pit vipers	26
Madagascan leaf-nosed snake	28
How snakes bite	30
Venom	32
Corn snake	34
Snake eyes	36
Black mamba	38
Garter snakes	40
Whip snakes	42
Sea snakes	44

CHAPTER 3

Snake spotting	46
Hognose snake	48
Coastal and inland taipan	50
Fer-de-lance	52
Emerald tree boa	54
Indian rock python	56
Green anaconda	58
King cobra	60
Rattlesnakes	62
Saw-scaled vipers	64
Péringuey's adder	66
Blind, or thread, snakes	68
Living with snakes	70

CHAPTER 1

The snake explorer's notebook

Turn the pages of this notebook to discover the world of snakes in sketches, words, and photographs.

This notebook records the amazing habits of snakes spotted in some of the world's most exciting places—from high mountains to steamy jungles and scorching deserts. It will introduce you to the world's longest and deadliest snakes, as well as the smallest and strangest ones. Do you think a snake can swallow a deer? Swim in the sea? Squeeze an alligator to death? Come along on an incredible snake-hunting journey to find the answers.

Northern ringneck snake

Sea snake

Snakes and dinosaurs

Fossil finds reveal that snakes evolved alongside their reptile relatives, the dinosaurs, some 167 million years ago.

The first snakes were long, lizardlike creatures with small back legs. As they evolved, they lost their legs, probably for easier burrowing.

Prehistoric snakes were carnivorous hunters with short, backward-curving teeth used for grabbing prey.

When an asteroid strike wiped out the dinosaurs 66 million years ago, snakes survived and over time evolved into today's snakes.

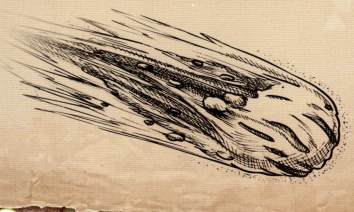

Titanoboa

Giant of the swamp

Titanoboa was the biggest-known snake ever! It measured about 43 feet (13 m) long (that's longer than a coach) and weighed 1.25 tons (1,135 kg)—the same as an average car. This giant water-loving snake lived about 60 million years ago. Its fossils were first found in Colombia, South America. It is an ancestor of living anacondas and boas.

Could a prehistoric snake eat a dinosaur?

Evidence suggests they did. A fossil of the Indian snake *Sanajeh indicus* was found coiled around a baby sauropod dinosaur.

Pythons were hunting in Europe about 45 million years ago, and fossils show they looked much like modern pythons.

Baby sauropod

Scores out of 10 — Titanoboa

Danger	Weight	Length	Speed
10	10	10	3

Modern royal python

Where in the world?

Like dinosaurs, snakes are reptiles, related to lizards, crocodiles, alligators, turtles, and tortoises.

After the dinosaurs died out 66 million years ago, more snake varieties began to develop and spread across the Earth. Today there are about 4,000 species living in Australia, Asia, Europe, Africa, and the Americas. There are none in Ireland or New Zealand, and none in Antarctica or Greenland, which are always cold. In places with cold winters, snakes survive by hibernating (going into a deep sleep), only waking up when warm spring weather arrives.

Sea snakes live in tropical oceans such as the Pacific and Indian Oceans. There are none in the cooler Atlantic Ocean.

Did you know?

Brazil has the most snake species (more than 400), while Australia has 20 of the 25 most dangerous venomous snakes. A venomous snake has a poison bite.

Banded sea krait

Hot desert snake, gwardar, or western brown snake

Some snakes live in unusual habitats, such as hot deserts or high mountains.

The main snake families are...
- Pythons
- Boas and anacondas
- Colubrids
- Vipers, pit vipers, and rattlesnakes
- Elapids

High mountain snake, Himalayan pit viper

Snake families include...
- Mole vipers
- Dwarf boas
- Round island ground boas, or split-jawed boas
- File, or elephant trunk
- Coral pipe
- Dwarf pipe
- Asian pipe
- Dawn blind
- Blind
- Slender blind, or thread
- Shield-tailed
- Mexican burrowing
- Sunbeam

Pythons

There are 40 species in the python family. They are originally from Africa, Asia, and Australia.

The longest python—and the world's longest snake—is the reticulated python, at more than 20 feet (6.25 m). That's longer than a giraffe is tall! The smallest is the pygmy python, at just 19.5 inches (50 cm)—similar in length to an adult cat.

Pythons (and boas) have kept some features found in the earliest snakes. For example, they have two lungs (most snakes have only one) and tiny, useless hind legs, like bony claws.

Reticulated python

Tiny hind leg

The ball or royal python lives in African grasslands and forests. It hunts at night for birds and small mammals, which are its main prey.

Fact File — Ball python

LENGTH:	5-6 feet (1.8 m)
WEIGHT:	up to 4.4 pounds (2 kg)
RANGE:	Africa

Scores out of 10

Danger	Weight	Length	Speed
2	4	5	2

When hunting, pythons use thermal receptors (organs that sense heat) around their mouth to detect body heat from prey.

When in danger, the ball python curls into a tight ball to protect its head and neck from attack.

This green tree python is using its thermal receptors to hunt.

A ball python curled into a ball.

11

Python habits

One good meal can last a python for months, or even a year!

Depending on their size, pythons may eat rats, lizards, monkeys, pigs, alligators, or even antelope. Like boas, pythons are constrictors—they coil their bodies around their prey and then constrict (squeeze) their muscles until the victim's heart and blood circulation stop, or it dies from internal damage. Then they swallow their prey whole!

Rock python constricting prey

Python moving slowly

Do pythons move fast?
No, they only reach 1 mph (1.6 km/h) on open ground—but since they ambush prey, they don't need to sprint.

Did you know?

Pythons can move almost in a straight line. They do this by stiffening their ribs, then lifting the scales on their belly and moving them forward so the ends grip the surface.

What should you do if a python wraps around you?
Don't panic—and unwind it from its tail to its head!

Boas

Boas are large, non-venomous snakes that hang from branches and ambush prey.

There are more than 40 species in the boa family. Most boas hunt on land. Like pythons, they kill by constriction—squeezing until the victim dies.

In the jungle, watch out for the boa constrictor. It can grow to more than 13 feet (3.9 m)—as long as two tall men lying end-to-end!

Boa constrictors are native to Central and South America, but also live wild in Florida, preying on birds, squirrels, reptiles, and even pet dogs.

After a large meal, a boa may not eat again for weeks.

Boa constrictor

Why does a boa flick out its forked tongue?

Like all snakes, a boa flicks out its tongue to "taste" scent particles in the air. When it pulls its tongue back in, a patch of sensory cells (the Jacobson's organ) "reads" the particles and sends signals to the brain, which can tell if a mate, or food, is close by.

Boas often sleep draped over branches.

Fact File — Boa constrictor

LENGTH: 13 feet (3.9 m)
WEIGHT: up to 100 pounds (45 kg)
RANGE: Americas

Scores out of 10

Danger	Weight	Length	Speed
5	8	8	2

Colubrids

About two-thirds of all snakes belong to the colubrid family— snakes that have no traces of legs and are mostly harmless.

There may be as many as 2,000 colubrid species, including garter, rat, milk, and grass snakes.

Although many colubrids are venomous (they inject poison), very few are dangerous to people. But take care if you spot the boomslang! Its venom is powerful enough to kill a human.

Britain's largest snake, the European grass snake, is also a colubrid. It preys on frogs, which it hunts in ponds and streams.

Can grass snakes swim underwater?
Yes! Grass snakes can hold their breath for more than 30 minutes.

Grass snake

Fact File
Grass snake

LENGTH: 3-5 feet (0.9-1.5 m)
WEIGHT: 8 ounces (225 g)
RANGE: Most of warmer Europe as far east as Crete (but not Ireland or Iceland)

Scores out of 10
Danger	Weight	Length	Speed
1	2	4	4

Do milk snakes drink cow's milk?

No! But it was once thought they did, because they are often found near farms, where they catch mice, frogs, and insects.

This boomslang is raiding a bird's nest.

Milk snake

Vipers

Watch out for vipers! These are some of the most dangerous snakes in the world.

There are about 200 species of vipers. The smallest are under 10 inches (25 cm) long, while the biggest—the bushmaster of Central and South America—is more than 10 feet (3 m) long, about the length of a kayak.

The viper family includes pit vipers, adders, and rattlesnakes, and they are all venomous—they inject venom (poison) through their fangs to paralyze and kill prey.

Blue viper

Beware a viper's stare! Their vertical pupils give these snakes better vision than most snakes, both in daylight and at night.

This gaboon viper (the biggest viper in Africa) is being "milked" for its venom, which is used to make anti-snakebite medicines.

Gaboon viper

You can spot a viper by its triangle-shaped head.

Fact File
Gaboon viper

LENGTH: 6 feet (1.8 m)
WEIGHT: 45 pounds (20 kg)
RANGE: Africa

Scores out of 10

Danger	Weight	Length	Speed
10	7	6	6

Elapids

Elapids are a family of venomous snakes with short fangs that are fixed, not hinged.

Most elapids are slim, fast hunters. When an elapid strikes, it stabs with a downward motion. About 60 of the 300 or so species of elapids live in Australia.

When competing for a mate, Australia's male tiger snakes will wrestle for hours, twisting their bodies around each other. The strongest one wins the female, who gives birth to as many as 30 snakelets.

The elapid family includes some of the most dangerous snakes in the world—cobras, coral snakes, mambas, kraits, and sea snakes.

Are elapids dangerous to humans?

Most elapids, such as the eastern coral snake of the southeastern United States, are rarely aggressive to people. However, the venom of some large elapids can be deadly, attacking the nervous system and causing paralysis (inability to move all or part of the body).

Eastern coral snake

Did you know?

Elapids, such as the tiger snake, use their short fangs to hang on to their prey and chew venom into their victim.

Fact File — Eastern tiger snake

LENGTH: 3–5 feet (1–1.5 m)
WEIGHT: 1.1 pounds (500 g)
RANGE: Australia and islands

Scores out of 10

Danger	Weight	Length	Speed
4	4	3	6

Tiger snake

Australia's death adder will sometimes try to ambush a giant cane toad to eat. Unfortunately for the snake, the cane toad has a poison in its skin that is strong enough to kill the death adder.

Cane toad

CHAPTER 2
Snake anatomy

The snakes in this chapter display some of the most interesting bodily features.

A snake has a very long, flexible backbone and many pairs of ribs.

The Malaysian blood python has a stout body for its short length, and looks unusually fat—it can weigh up to 20 pounds (9 kg)!

Malaysian blood python

Snake skeleton

Did you know?

All snakes are cold-blooded—their body temperature is the same as the temperature of their environment.

Most snakes have overlapping scales.

Can snakes blink?

No! They don't have eyelids, so they can't blink. Snakes sleep with their eyes open.

Rhinoceros viper

European blind snake

Some of the world's snakes are weird and wonderful.

The rhinoceros viper from central Africa, for example, has a horn on its nose!

In contrast, tiny blind snakes are smooth and thin, and feed on ants. At just 12 inches (30 cm), they are no longer than a school ruler.

Reticulated python

Most snakes have long bodies, but the record-breaker was a reticulated python found in 1912. It measured 33 feet (10 m) from nose to tail—about the same as the height of a three-story building!

Reticulated pythons get their name from the diamond-shaped pattern on their skin ("reticulated" means "netlike"). These big snakes are active hunters, preying on anything from bats to pigs. The python usually seizes its prey by the head and coils around it to kill it in under four minutes. Swallowing may take an hour, and digestion may take several weeks.

Reticulated python

A big reticulated python can swallow a human! As in all snakes, its upper and lower jaws are split into two parts (left side and right side), so the jaw can stretch extra wide.

Did you know?

Female reticulated pythons are bigger than males. They need extra body space to hold their eggs.

A reticulated python can open its mouth to 180 degrees!

Fact File — Reticulated python

LENGTH: up to 33 feet (10 m)
WEIGHT: 165 pounds (75 kg)
RANGE: Southeast Asia

Scores out of 10

Danger	Weight	Length	Speed
6	8	10	3

Pit vipers

Pit vipers hunt in the dark using heat sensors.

Some (but not all) vipers, pythons, and boas have holes on their faces called "pits." These contain heat-sensing organs that detect heat from warm bodies. The pits act like night-vision goggles, helping the snake to "see" a heat image of a predator or prey in total darkness up to 3 feet (1 m) away.

Wagler's pit viper

Bushmaster

Well-known pit viper species include the bushmaster, fer-de-lance, rattlesnake, moccasin, and copperhead.

The pit is between the and nostril.

Moccasin

Eastern copperhead

A pit viper's large eyes pick up the slightest movement close to the snake.

Did you know?

When hunting, pit vipers keep very still, so as not to alert the prey, then they move at speed to strike with their poison fangs and secure a meal.

Pit vipers, such as this white-lipped pit viper, should never be approached.

Fact File
Wagler's pit viper

LENGTH: female 3.2 feet (1 m)
male 2.4 feet (75 cm)

WEIGHT: female 1-2 pounds (up to 1 kg)
male 8 ounces (225 g)

RANGE: Southeast Asia

Scores out of 10

Danger 4 Weight 3 Length 3 Speed 2

Madagascan leaf-nosed snake

In the jungles of Madagascar, this snake appears to look like part of the forest to avoid being seen by prey.

Madagascan leaf-nosed snake

Females have a nose that looks like a frayed leaf, while in males it is long and straight. This snake can even bend its nose! No one quite knows why, but it aids the snake's superb camouflage among forest leaves.

The Madagascan leaf-nosed snake lies in wait for a frog or small lizard, and when its prey is very close, it strikes at lightning speed.

Ranomafana National Park, Madagascar

What is being done to help this snake survive?

Many areas have been made into national parks and reserves, which provide safe places for this snake to live.

Most snakes use "camouflage"—their skin colors or patterns help them blend in with their surroundings—but the Madagascan leaf-nosed snake hangs stiffly upside-down from a branch so it looks like a seed pod!

Snake or seed pod?

Did you know?
In all snakes the scales are made of a hard substance called keratin, just like human fingernails. The scales overlap and move as the snake moves.

Nose like a frayed leaf

Fact File
Madagascan leaf-nosed snake

LENGTH: 2.3 feet (70 cm)
WEIGHT: 0.1 ounce (2 g)
RANGE: Madagascar

Madagascar

Scores out of 10

Danger: 0
Weight: 1
Length: 3
Speed: 7

How snakes bite

When a snake shows its teeth, it's time to back off!

Snake teeth curve backward and are designed for seizing prey and pulling it into the snake's throat, so the snake can swallow it whole. Only venomous snakes have fangs—long, hollow, or grooved teeth connected to a venom sac behind the snake's eyes.

Most snakes do not inject venom (poison), but even non-venomous snakes have strong teeth and a bite can leave a nasty wound.

An Indian python with its jaws wide open.

Snake jaws are strong and very flexible, which is why snakes can swallow prey much larger than themselves.

Backward-pointing teeth provide good grip on prey.

Old teeth constantly break away from a snake's jaw and new teeth take their place.

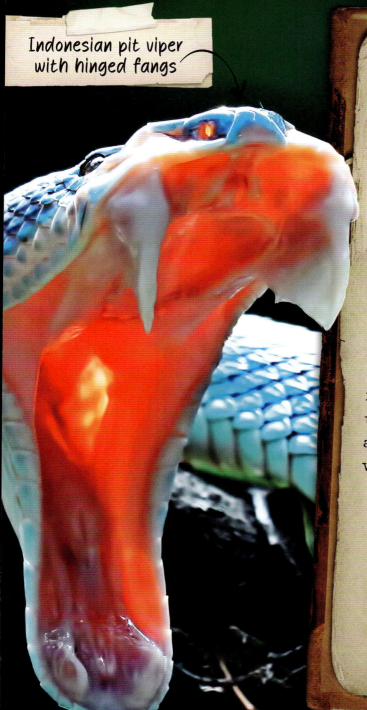

Indonesian pit viper with hinged fangs

Different snakes have different types of teeth

Aglyph snakes have non-venomous, backward-facing teeth and no fangs.

boas, rat snakes, and kingsnakes

Opisthoglyph snakes have grooved fangs at the back of the mouth. The snake releases venom as it chews prey.

hog-nosed snakes

Proteroglyph snakes have fixed (non-hinged), solid teeth. The snake strikes and hangs on while the venom kills the prey.

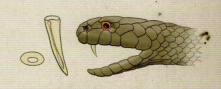

cobras, coral snakes, and sea snakes

Solenoglyph snakes have hinged fangs that lie flat when the mouth is shut. The snake strikes, injects venom, releases, then hunts down the injured prey.

vipers and rattlesnakes

Venom

About 600 snake species are venomous—they use poison to kill their prey.

Snake venom is made by organs like our salivary (spit) glands. Saliva helps us digest food, but in venomous snakes, it contains poisonous enzymes (substances that control chemical reactions).

To be effective, venom must enter the victim's bloodstream. Most snakes, such as pit vipers, simply punch holes in their prey as they bite, and venom flows into the wound. But a few venomous snakes, such as rattlesnakes, inject their venom through hollow fangs.

Six very venomous snakes to avoid...

A black mamba's venom attacks nerves, paralyzing the victim.

The saw-scaled viper kills the most humans!

The aggressive saw-scaled viper bites often.

Snake venom works fastest on prey animals, such as rodents.

The fer-de-lance is extremely venomous.

The venom glands (modified salivary glands) are located just behind and below the eye.

Venom gland

The king cobra's venom can kill humans in two to six hours.

The yellow-bellied sea snake is Hawaii's most venomous snake.

The inland taipan has the most deadly venom.

The taipan's venom **paralyzes muscles,** stops breathing, and damages blood vessels.

Did you know?

Venomous snakes are most dangerous to people when the snakes live near villages and cities.

Corn snake

The corn snake is a type of rat snake. It is known as the farmer's friend because it preys on rats that eat corn.

Corn snakes are good hunters and are not venomous. Like boas, they are constrictors. First, they bite their prey to get a firm grip with their backward-pointing teeth, then they coil around the victim and squeeze.

Swallowing begins as soon as the prey has stopped struggling. The food is usually swallowed head-first, often still alive!

Snakelet hatching

Corn snake eggs take 60 to 70 days to hatch.

Fact File — Corn snake

LENGTH: 6 feet (1.8 m)
WEIGHT: 2 pounds (0.9 kg)
RANGE: North America

Scores out of 10

Danger	Weight	Length	Speed
1	3	6	4

Some people keep corn snakes as pets.

When it feels threatened, a corn snake vibrates its tail.

Tail rattling is often followed by a bite!

Corn snake

Snake eyes

You can't out-stare a snake! Unlike a lizard, a snake cannot blink. Its eyes are always open.

Most snakes are good at spotting movements close by, such as prey to catch, or an enemy to escape from.

Snakes that hunt during the day have eye lenses that act as sunglasses, filtering out ultraviolet light (invisible shortwave light rays) to sharpen their vision. The eyes of night-hunting snakes have lenses that let in ultraviolet light, to help the snake see in the dark.

A snake's stare was once thought to hypnotize. There is no scientific evidence for this.

The spectacle makes the eye look glassy.

A snake's eye is protected from dust by a clear scale, called a "spectacle," which is fixed in place.

Boomslang

The snake-haired Medusa of Greek myth turned anyone who met her gaze to stone.

Eye types

The pupil (the black part) of a snake's eye gives clues to the snake's lifestyle.

Tree and vine snakes have horizontal pupils and narrow snouts, so they can see straight ahead.

Night hunters, such as vipers, boas, and pythons, have vertical pupils that look like slits.

Snakes that hunt by day, such as the boomslang, have large eyes and round pupils.

Western bush viper

Sri Lankan green vine snake

Boomslang

Black mamba

This very long, very fast snake can be very aggressive.

Watch out for the shy but dangerous black mamba in Africa's rocky savannas and lowland forests, south of the Sahara Desert.

At up to 14 feet (4.3 m) long, the black mamba is the longest venomous snake in Africa, and the fastest land snake in the world!

One bite from a black mamba contains enough venom to kill 15 people!

Black mamba

The black mamba can strike in a fraction of a second.

How fast can a black mamba move?

This snake can travel up to 12.5 mph (20 km/h) for a short distance. Humans have an average running speed of 6 mph (9.6 km/h), so only a trained athlete could be confident of outrunning this snake!

A warning hiss means "stay away!"

Fact File — Black mamba

LENGTH: 14 feet (4.3 m)
WEIGHT: 3.5 pounds (1.5 kg)
RANGE: Africa

Scores out of 10

Danger	Weight	Length	Speed
10	3	8	10

A black mamba will strike repeatedly.

Did you know?

Only the inside of a mamba's mouth is black. Its body is gray to brownish-green.

A black mamba's power comes from the muscles attached to its ribs and spine. These give it its whippy movement across the ground and its incredible strike speed.

Garter snakes

Like all snakes, garter snakes are cold-blooded, which means they cannot make their own body heat.

Their bodies need to be warmed by the sun to work properly. During cold winters, when there isn't much sun, they survive by hibernating (going into a deep sleep).

From late October, garter snakes look for a safe place to hibernate, often beneath old logs, rocks, or in crayfish burrows on riverbanks. Hundreds of garter snakes may hibernate together.

Did you know?
Garter snakes are not venomous, but can produce a nasty odor when alarmed.

How do garter snakes hunt?
Garter snakes hunt mainly during the day, often near water. You may see them raising their heads and peering to spot prey, which they ambush, then swallow whole.

A forked tongue collects scent particles from two places at once.

Garter snakes in a huddle

In spring, garter snakes wake from hibernation and hunt frogs, mice, and worms to eat.

Common garter snake

Fact File
Common garter snake

LENGTH: 3 feet (0.9 m)
WEIGHT: 5 ounces (150 g)
RANGE: North America

Scores out of 10

Danger	Weight	Length	Speed
1	2	3	5

41

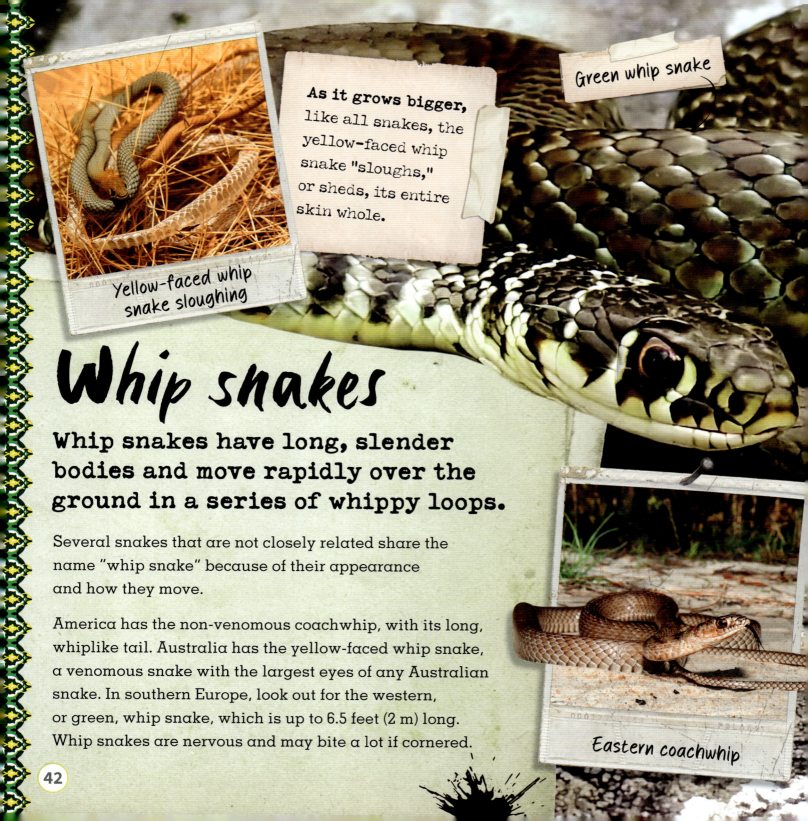

Yellow-faced whip snake sloughing

As it grows bigger, like all snakes, the yellow-faced whip snake "sloughs," or sheds, its entire skin whole.

Green whip snake

Whip snakes

Whip snakes have long, slender bodies and move rapidly over the ground in a series of whippy loops.

Several snakes that are not closely related share the name "whip snake" because of their appearance and how they move.

America has the non-venomous coachwhip, with its long, whiplike tail. Australia has the yellow-faced whip snake, a venomous snake with the largest eyes of any Australian snake. In southern Europe, look out for the western, or green, whip snake, which is up to 6.5 feet (2 m) long. Whip snakes are nervous and may bite a lot if cornered.

Eastern coachwhip

Do snakes share their nests?

Yes! The yellow-faced whip snake sometimes lays eggs in shared nests containing up to 600 eggs.

Fact File — Yellow-faced whip snake

LENGTH: up to 3.3 feet (up to 1 m)
WEIGHT: 3.5–7 ounces (100–200 g)
RANGE: Australia

Scores out of 10

Danger	Weight	Length	Speed
3	2	2	5

Yellow-faced whip snake

Whip snakes are active hunters during the day. They have large eyes and good eyesight.

Sea snakes

Sea snakes live in tropical oceans.

There are two groups of sea snakes—true sea snakes and sea kraits.

True sea snakes have flattened bodies with paddlelike tails for swimming. Their young are born underwater from eggs inside the female.

Sea kraits are amphibious, which means they are good swimmers, but can also crawl, climb, and lay eggs on land.

What do sea snakes drink? Not salty seawater, because too much salt is bad for them! Instead, they drink fresh water, either from rain, or by coming ashore.

Banded sea krait

Scales don't overlap!

Land snakes have overlapping scales to protect their bodies from getting scraped on the ground, but most sea snakes don't need this type of protection. Instead, their scales butt up to each other like tiles on a floor.

True sea snake

Sea snake near a popular beach

Sea snakes have the most potent venom of any snake. But their short fangs deliver only a small amount of venom, so a bite from a sea snake is seldom a danger to people.

Did you know?

Most sea snakes visit the surface every 30 minutes or so to breathe. However, some true sea snakes can stay underwater for up to eight hours. That's because they absorb 33 percent of the oxygen they need through their skin.

Fact File — Banded sea krait

LENGTH: male 2.8 feet (85 cm), female 4.6 feet (140 cm)

WEIGHT: male under 2 pounds (0.9 kg), female up to 4 pounds (1.8 kg)

RANGE: Indian and Pacific Oceans

Scores out of 10

Danger: 3
Weight: 4
Length: 5
Speed: 4

CHAPTER 3

Snake spotting

You can spot snakes not just in the wild, but also living surprisingly close to people.

In warm countries, such as India and Australia, you can sometimes find snakes inside houses. They like to crawl under floors and roofs. They also like to hide in outbuildings or in warm compost heaps.

In the wild, look for snakes sunbathing on rocks, swimming in streams and lakes, hiding in hollow tree trunks or piles of leaves, or slithering through long grass. Snakes usually sense us long before we spot them.

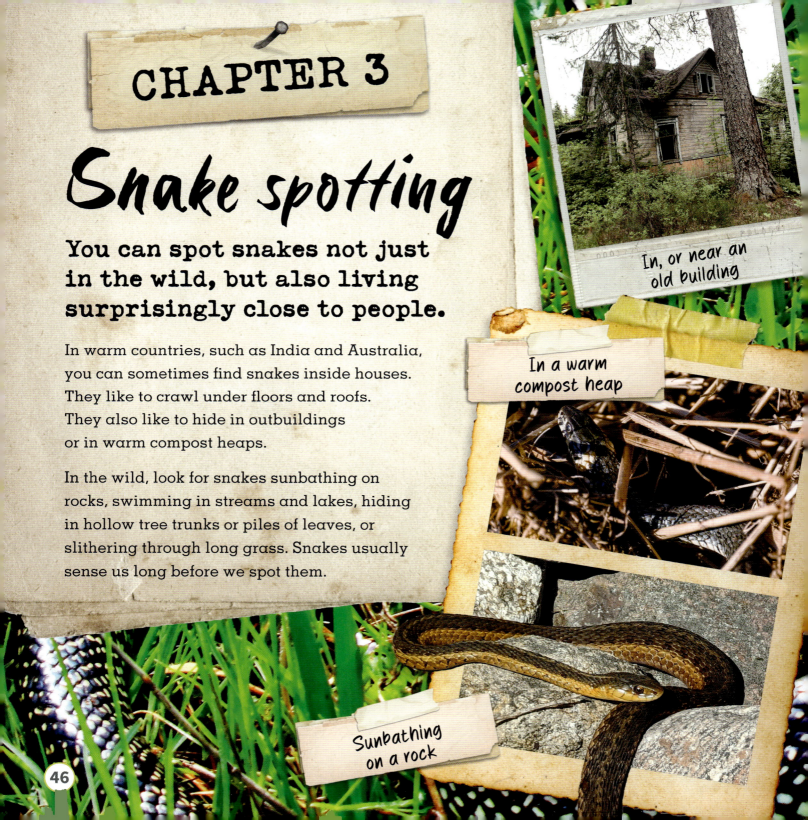

In, or near an old building

In a warm compost heap

Sunbathing on a rock

Fishing in a lake

Slithering through long grass

Camouflaged in dry leaves

Hiding in a tree trunk

Hognose snake

"Hognose snake" is the name given to several unrelated species with upturned snouts.

North America's eastern hognose snake has a clever way to put off predators. If threatened, instead of trying to hide or escape, first it hisses and flattens its neck to make itself look bigger, like a cobra. Then, if this doesn't work, it rolls over with its mouth open and "plays dead," hoping the predator will lose interest.

Like some other snakes, the hognose snake can produce a nasty smell when scared, or threatened.

Did you know?

Snakes hiss to scare off predators, not to communicate with other snakes. They have an organ in the throat called the glottis. When they push air out with force, structures in the glottis rattle and make a hissing sound.

The eastern hognose snake prefers sandy soils that it can burrow into.

Fact File — Eastern hognose snake

LENGTH: female 2.6 feet (80 cm), male 2 feet (60 cm)
WEIGHT: female 1 pound (450 g), male less than 1 pound (450 g)
RANGE: North America

Scores out of 10

Danger	Weight	Length	Speed
0	3	3	2

Hognose snake "playing dead"

Flattening its neck makes the snake look bigger and scarier.

Why do hognose snakes have an upturned snout?

For digging out toads, a favorite meal!

Coastal and inland taipan

The coastal taipan is one of Australia's deadliest snakes.

One particular coastal taipan living in the Australian Reptile Park holds the world record for producing the most venom at one time. Scientists at the park extracted enough venom from this snake to kill 400 people!

The inland taipan is slightly smaller, but just as deadly. Both types prey on birds and small mammals, such as rats.

Extracting venom to make antivenom

Coastal taipan

Did you know?

Taipan venom can kill a person in 30 minutes. To survive, a bite victim must take antivenom within that time.

Taipans and other venomous snakes are kept in captivity, so their venom can be extracted. Snake venom is used to make antivenom (medicines that counteract the effects of venom). Antivenoms can save the lives of snakebite victims.

Fact File — Coastal taipan

LENGTH: 9.5 feet (2.9 m)
WEIGHT: 14.5 pounds (6.5 kg)
RANGE: Australia

Scores out of 10

Danger	Weight	Length	Speed
10	6	8	9

Inland taipan

How do taipans hunt?

When a taipan detects the movement of a rat, it "freezes," then strikes and bites at incredible speed. It then lets the rat move away to die, so as not to get bitten itself.

Fer-de-lance

The fer-de-lance, or "lance head," is one of the most feared of all snakes.

In Central America, the fer-de-lance—a pit viper—causes more human deaths than any other snake. Camouflaged to look like dry leaves, it lurks on sugar and coffee plantations.

South American relatives of the fer-de-lance live in grasslands and forests, often near lakes and rivers. They include the jararaca and the jumping viper, which leaps into the air as it bites.

Jumping viper

Jararaca

Does the fer-de-lance lay eggs?

No! The female fer-de-lance gives birth to as many as 50 hungry snakelets (baby snakes) in one night.

Fer-de-lance

Did you know?
The fer-de-lance has a clever trick. It will curl a leaf over its body to hide itself as it waits for prey.

The fer-de-lance can live to be more than 20 years old. Pythons generally live to be 30 years, while garter snakes only live three to four years.

Fact File — Fer de lance

LENGTH: 7 feet (2 m)
WEIGHT: 13 pounds (6 kg)
RANGE: Central and South America

Scores out of 10

Danger	Weight	Length	Speed
10	4	7	9

Emerald tree boa

As it grows, a young emerald tree boa turns from orange, or red, to emerald green.

In the rainforests of South America, the green adults are hard to spot among the leaves. They hang from branches, jaws gaping, ready to seize passing prey, such as rats, bats, lizards, and small mammals.

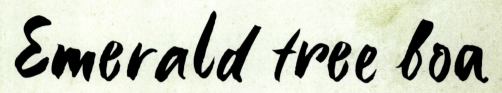

Young emerald tree boa

How does the emerald tree boa hunt?

It lies in wait, bites, constricts (squeezes), and then swallows. Acids in the snake's stomach digest the meal. This can take days, or even weeks!

Lying in wait for prey

The emerald tree boa has heat-sensitive pits (holes) along its upper and lower lips that detect heat from the bodies of other animals.

Fact File — Emerald tree boa

LENGTH:	6 feet (1.8 m)
WEIGHT:	3.3 pounds (1.5 kg)
RANGE:	South America

Scores out of 10

Danger	Weight	Length	Speed
2	4	5	3

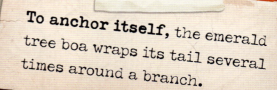

To anchor itself, the emerald tree boa wraps its tail several times around a branch.

Heat-sensitive pits along lips

The tail is "prehensile" (able to grasp).

Indian rock python

This snake was the inspiration for Kaa in Rudyard Kipling's *The Jungle Book*.

The Indian rock python, also called the Indian python, is solitary (it lives on its own), except during the mating season. It hunts at night, either on the ground or in trees, and is also at home in water.

Although large, the Indian rock python is rarely aggressive, even if attacked. It captures prey by striking, biting, and constricting (squeezing) until the victim dies.

Albino pythons lack brown and black on their skin

Did you know?

Female Indian rock pythons first warm their bodies in the sun, then coil around their eggs to keep them warm.

Indian rock python

A rock python is as long as three baseball bats placed end to end!

Fact File — Indian rock python

LENGTH: 20 feet (6 m)
WEIGHT: 300 pounds (137 kg)
RANGE: India

Scores out of 10

Danger	Weight	Length	Speed
5	9	8	2

This snake eats prey as big as deer!

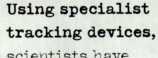

Using specialist tracking devices, scientists have figured out that a rock python's home range, the area where it lives and hunts) is about 1.6 square miles (4.2 sq km). That's slightly bigger than Central Park in New York City!

Green anaconda

This huge, heavy snake may be lurking just below the water!

Anacondas are large South American snakes. The green anaconda is the biggest of the four species.

This massive boa often hunts at night, hiding almost submerged in a slow-moving river. It kills fish and turtles by biting. It also coils itself around large prey such as a tapir, wild pig, or caiman, and squeezes until the victim's heart stops beating. Then it swallows it whole.

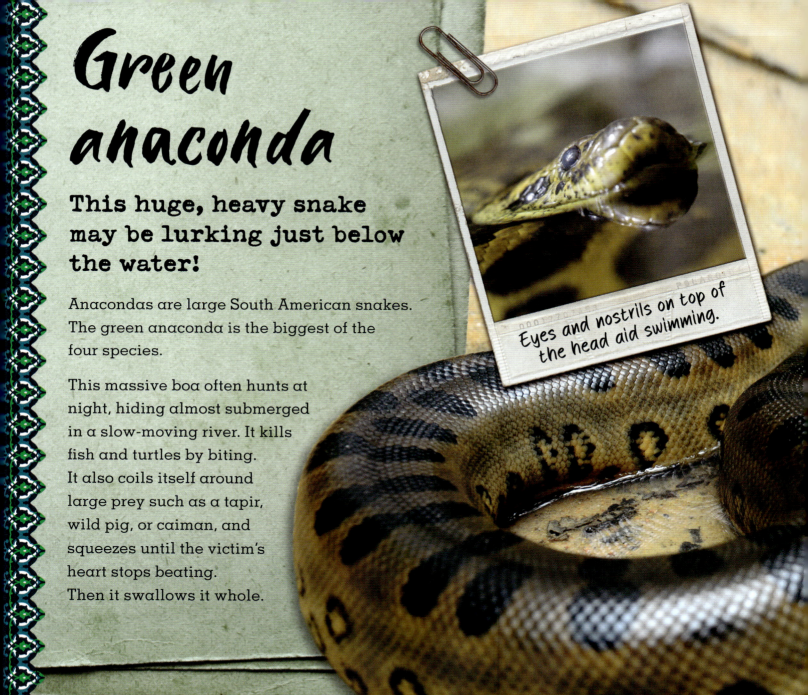

Eyes and nostrils on top of the head aid swimming.

Green anaconda

Did you know?

The green anaconda is the heaviest snake in the world! At 550 pounds (250 kg), it weighs as much as three grown men!

Fact File — Green anaconda

LENGTH: over 29 feet (9 m)
WEIGHT: 550 pounds (250 kg)
RANGE: South American rivers, including the Amazon River, and Trinidad

Scores out of 10

Danger	Weight	Length	Speed
8	9	9	5

Predators

Not many creatures can take on an anaconda—but a jaguar can! It catches and eats yellow anacondas (a close relative of the green anaconda).

King cobra

Venomous snakes don't get much bigger than this!

Watch out for the king cobra—it's the longest venomous snake, and its bite contains a poison that can be deadly to humans. When threatened, a king cobra rears up and extends the ribs in its neck area to give it a fearsome hood, which makes it look even bigger. Its excellent eyesight and vibration-sensing body allow it to track prey—almost always other snakes!

King cobra

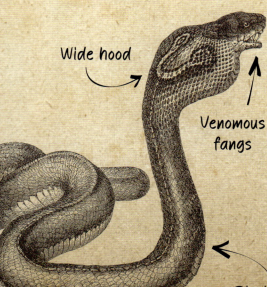

Wide hood

Venomous fangs

Distinctive pattern

Did you know?

King cobras may be dangerous, but they're very shy of humans! You're unlikely to see one in the wild.

Fact File

LENGTH: Up to 18 feet (5.6 m)
WEIGHT: Up to 28 pounds (12.7 kg)
RANGE: Northern India, southern China, the Malay Peninsula, western Indonesia

Scores out of 10

Danger	Weight	Length	Speed
10	8	8	8

Deadly Bite

The king cobra has some of the most deadly venom of any reptile. One bite contains enough neurotoxin to kill an elephant, or 20 people.

Beware the king cobra's deadly bite!

Rattlesnakes

Rattlesnakes are named for the scaly "rattle" at the tip of their tails.

Rattlesnakes shake their rattle to warn off predators—the sound means "don't mess with me"! A rattlesnake can strike faster than you can blink your eye!

More than 30 species live in the Americas, from Canada to Argentina. One of the best known is the eastern diamondback. At up to 8 feet (2.4 m) long, it is America's largest venomous snake.

Did you know?

A rattlesnake can twitch its tail muscles up to 90 times a second. This makes the hard, loose segments at the tip of its tail rattle.

Rattlesnakes inject venom through their hollow fangs. As well as killing prey, the venom helps with digestion.

Mojave rattlesnake

Rattle

The sidewinder rattlesnake moves rapidly across hot sand. To stop it from overheating, only two points on its body touch the ground at any one time.

Sidewinder rattlesnake

Eastern diamondback rattlesnake

Fact File — Eastern diamondback

LENGTH: 8 feet (2.4 m)
WEIGHT: 5 pounds (2.3 kg)
RANGE: North America

Scores out of 10

Danger	Weight	Length	Speed
9	5	7	8

Saw-scaled vipers

Small but deadly, these aggressive vipers live in dry parts of Africa, southwest Asia, and India.

The eight species of saw-scaled viper hunt mammals, lizards, frogs, insects—and even other snakes! When disturbed, they slither their body into a moving crescent shape, and as their scales rub against each other, they make a rasping sound—a warning to others to stay well clear!

When a saw-scaled viper attacks, it bites multiple times, making it extremely dangerous. Thousands of people in India die each year from its bites.

Saw-scaled vipers have large eyes with vertical pupils, typical of snakes that hunt at night.

An Indian saw-scaled viper hunting at night.

Saw-scaled viper striking

Fact File — Saw-scaled viper

LENGTH: 3 feet (0.9 m)
WEIGHT: 14 ounces (400 g)
RANGE: Africa, southwest Asia, India

Scores out of 10

Danger	Weight	Length	Speed
10	2	2	7

Did you know?
The scales along the lower body have a serrated (jagged) edge, like the blade of a saw.

Saw-scaled viper in warning position

The serrated scales stick out rather than lie flat.

Péringuey's adder

Péringuey's adder lives in the Namib Desert of southwest Africa.

To hunt, this venomous viper, also known as the desert sidewinding adder, buries itself in soft sand, with only its eyes and the tip of its tail showing. Then it waits for a lizard, or gecko, to come close, and pounces.

To minimize contact with the hot sand, Péringuey's adder moves in sideways loops, so that only a small part of its body touches the sand at any one time. This leaves a distinctive track.

How does this snake get enough water to survive?

By eating lizards with a high water content.

This Péringuey's adder is about to swallow a large lizard.

The position of this snake's eyes are higher on its head than most snake eyes.

When buried in sand, only the eyes of the Péringuey's adder are visible.

Péringuey's adder

Fact File — Péringuey's adder

LENGTH:	up to 0.8 feet (up to 25 cm)
WEIGHT:	0.7–1.0 ounce (20–30 g)
RANGE:	Namib Desert, southwest Africa

Scores out of 10

Danger	Weight	Length	Speed
1	2	2	4

Blind, or thread, snakes

These unusual snakes live underground.

Blind, or thread, snakes are burrowers that look like worms and live mostly in warm soil. They range in size from just 4 inches (10 cm) to about 3 feet (90 cm) long. They feed mainly on the eggs and larvae of ants and termites, which they find by following chemical scent-trails left by the adult insects.

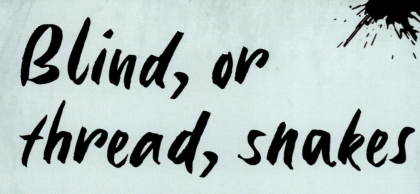

Blind snakes only emerge from underground at dusk or at night.

The Brahminy blind snake is as thin as a noodle. It is also known as the flowerpot snake, because it often hides in flowerpots.

Do blind snakes have eyes?

Yes and no! Before they are born, they have eyes, but by the time they are born, their eyes have reduced to dots and they are born blind.

European blind snake

Fact File — Brahminy blind snake

LENGTH (average): 4 inches (10 cm)
WEIGHT: 0.02 ounce (0.6 g)
RANGE: Worldwide

Scores out of 10

Danger	Weight	Length	Speed
0	1	1	1

All Brahminy blind snakes are females. The offspring develop in eggs that have not been fertilized by a male—a process called "parthenogenesis."

Blind snake swallowing a grub.

Blind snakes cannot open their jaws wide. Some snatch prey and swallow, while others suck out the juicy insides of their meal.

Living with snakes

Some snakes have adapted to life alongside us, but human activities threaten many species.

In many parts of the world, these beautiful creatures are in danger, killed out of fear, or for their skins, for food, or for use in traditional medicines. Live snakes are also smuggled and traded illegally.

But one thing snakes have shown us over millions of years is that they are survivors!

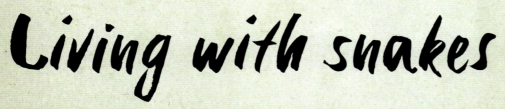

What is the biggest threat to snakes?

Loss of habitat, such as forests and grasslands, is the biggest threat. In many countries these natural habitats are being cleared to make way for farms, plantations, and cities.

Did you know?

Most snakes are harmless, but if you do find a snake, **do not try to pick it up.** About 100,000 people die from snake venom every year.

What can we do to help save snakes?

Slow down when driving in snakey places. Lots of snakes are killed by cars.

Restore and protect snake habitats.

Use less pesticides (such as ant poison) and herbicides (weed killers), which are toxic to snakes.

Make yards wildlife friendly by leaving fallen logs or rocks in place and providing ground-level fresh water.

Snakes are helpful predators of rats, mice, and other farm pests.

Rat-catcher!

Picture credits

The publishers would like to thank Shutterstock for their kind permission to reproduce the pictures in this book.

Breck P. Kent 1; Audrey Snider-Bell 2L, (author unknown) 2TR, reptiles4all 2BR, patternsearch 2-3BG, Artpose Adam Borkowski 3TL (and other pages), Marc Freebrey 3TR, Jay Ondreicka 4TR, NadyGinzburg 4BR, [notebook] 4-5, Markparker1983 5TL, Lauren Suryanata 5BL, Ralfa Padantya 5C, Marc Freebrey 5TR, Ken Griffiths 5CR, FeatherStalker Don 5BR; pikepicture 6BL, Michael Rosskothen 6-7, Morphart Creation 7TL, tdal 7TR, Egoreichenkov Evgenii 7BR; Rich Carey 8BR, saam3rd 8-9, (author unknown) 9TL, (author unknown) 9BR; Ken Griffiths 10B, I Wayan Sumatika 10-11, Kurit afshen 11BL, Opayaza12 11BR; VIVEK HARISH RAUT 12BL, Nick Greaves 12-13, Yatra4289 13TL; (author unknown) 14BL, Jan Hejda 14-15, 24Novembers 15BL, Susan Flashman 15TR; mar_chm1982 16BR, Marc Freebrey 16-17, (author unknown) 17BL, FotoRequest 17BR, Mark_Kostich 18B, (author unknown) 18-19, Lauren Suryanata 19BL, Zoran zoo-vrt 19TR; Jay Ondreicka 20BR, (author unknown) 20-21, Al Carrera 21BR; dwi putra stock 22BL, jeep2499 22-23, Zsolyomi 23BL, Stefano Buttafoco 23TR, RMMPPhotography 23CR; TamuT 24-25, mijicals 25BL, bluedog studio 25TR; (author unknown) 26CL, Seth LaGrange 26BL, (author unknown) 26BC, Scott Delony 26R, DSlight_photography 26-27, haryanta.p 27BL; Danny Ye 28-29 (main), goran_safarek 28-29 (small), Vladislav T. Jirousek 29T, reptiles4all 29BL, Rawpixel.com 29BR; PUMPZA 30BL, (author unknown) 30TR, Agus_Gatam 30-31, Amadeu Blasco 31R (x4); Sheril Kannoth 32BL, Craig Cordier 32CR, Jim Cumming 32BR, patternsearch 32-33, (author unknown) 33TL, NickEvansKZN 33BL, Ken Griffiths 33C, Dream Frame Photography 33TR, Free Line 33BR; bluedog studio 34B, Jan Hejda 34-35 (main), TAMER YILMAZ 34-35 (small), Morphart Creation 35TR, Struppi 35B; Asmus Koefoed 36BL, Pedro Hamilton Oliveira 36TR, Mayanur Akter 36-37, Chamod Gunathilake 37BL, Lauren Suryanata 37C, Dima Moroz 37TR, Eugene Troskie 37BR; (author unknown) 38BL, Craig Cordier 38-39, Craig Cordier 39TL, reptiles4all 39BL, Craig Cordier 39CR; Rogney Piedra Arencibia 40BR, Aaron of L.A. Photography 40-41, Christina Dutkowski 41T; Ken Griffiths 42TL, Jay Ondreicka 42BR, Swaroop Pixs 42-43, Bodor Tivadar 43TL, Ken Griffiths 43BL, Morphart Creation 43TR; Arturo Vigil 44BL, Rich Carey 44R, Gti861 44-45, Tomas Kotouc 45TL, Damsea 45TR; Svetliy 46TR, Uzo Borewicz 46CR, (author unknown) 46BR, Daniel Koglin 46-47, Esteban Sanchez 47TL, Sebastian_Photography 47BC, Mark F Lotterhand 47BR; Mike Wilhelm 48BR, Joe Farah 48-49, Mike Wilhelm 49BL, (author unknown) 49BR; Elnur 50TR, reptiles4all 50BR, Ken Griffiths 50-51; BMJ 52TR, Tacio Philip Sansonovski 52BR, Agami Photo Agency 52-53, Thorsten Spoerlein 53CL; Marlon Aguero Photography 54B, Audrey Snider-Bell 54-55, (author unknown) 55BL, Breck P. Kent 55BR; (author unknown) 56BC, Alexey Pevnev 56TR, PinkeshTanna 56-57, Padodo 57TL, T photography 57BL, Pandey Abhinav 57R; MattiaATH 58TR, Patrick K. Campbell 58-59; [vintage pic] 60BL, [king cobra main pic] 60-61, [deadly bite] 61BL, [vintage trees] 61TR; Maria Dryfhout 62BR, Rusty Dodson 62-63, Mark F Lotterhand 63BR, 1469852024 63TR; reptiles4all 64BR, (author unknown) 64-65, NileshShah 65TL, Luis Montero de Espinosa 65BR; Stefan Scharf 66BR, Chantelle Bosch 66-67 (small), AZ Outdoor Photography 66-67 (main), Chantelle Bosch 67TR; AVA Bitter 68BL, TAMER YILMAZ 68TR, Simlinger 68-69, Dr.MYM 69BL, muhamad mizan bin ngateni 69R; Tarcisio Schnaider 70BL, Miguel Prs 70-71, Lauren Suryanata 71B; Rich Carey 72 TL, Rogney Piedra Arencibia 72B, Audrey Snider-Bell 72R, patternsearch 72BG.